Great Gospel Favorites

Contents

ISBN 0-634-00599-5

HAL•LEONARD®
CORPORATION
7777 W. BLUEMOUND RD. P.O. BOX 13819 MILWAUKEE, WI 53213

Visit Hal Leonard Online at
www.halleonard.com

AMAZING GRACE

Words by JOHN NEWTON
Traditional American Melody

taught my heart to fear and grace my fears re-lieved.
prom-ised good to me, His word my hope se-cures.

How pre-cious did that grace ap-pear the
He will my shield and por-tion be as

hour I first be-lieved. 2. Through
long as life en-dures.

Verse 3
And when this flesh and heart shall fail
and mortal life shall cease.
I shall possess within the veil
a life of joy and peace.

When we've been there ten thousand years,
bright shining as the sun.

We've no less days to sing God's praise
than when we first begun.

ARE YOU WASHED IN THE BLOOD

Traditional

1. Have you been to Je - sus for the cleans - ing pow'r? Are you
2.-4. *(See additional lyrics)*

washed in the blood of the Lamb? Are you full - y trust-ing in His

grace this hour? Are you washed in the blood of the Lamb? Are you

Refrain

Additional Lyrics

2. Are you walking daily by the Savior's side?
    Are you washed in the blood of the Lamb?
    Do you rest each moment in the Crucified?
    Are you washed in the blood of the Lamb?
    REFRAIN

3. When the Bridegroom cometh will your robes be white?
    Are you washed in the blood of the Lamb?
    Will your soul be ready for the mansions bright,
    And be washed in the blood of the Lamb?
    REFRAIN

4. Lay aside the garments that are stained with sin,
    And be washed in the blood of the Lamb;
    There's a fountain flowing for the soul unclean,
    O be washed in the blood of the Lamb!
    REFRAIN

AT CALVARY

Words by WILLIAM NEWELL
Music by D.B. TOWNE

1. Years I spent in van-i-ty and pride,
2.-4. *(See additional lyrics)*

Car-ing not my Lord was cru-ci-fied, Know-ing not it was for me He died On Cal-va-ry.

Mer - cy there was great, and grace was free; Par - don there was mul - ti -
plied to me; There my bur - dened soul found lib - er - ty At
Cal - va - ry. ry.

Additional Lyrics

2. By God's Word at last my sin I learned;
Then I trembled at the law I'd spurned,
Till my guilty soul imploring turned To Calvary.
REFRAIN

3. Now I've giv'n to Jesus ev'rything,
Now I gladly own Him as my King,
Now my raptured soul can only sing Of Calvary.
REFRAIN

4. Oh, the love that drew salvation's plan!
Oh, the grace that bro't it down to man!
Oh, the mighty gulf that God did span At Calvary.
REFRAIN

BLESSED ASSURANCE

Lyrics by FANNY CROSBY and VAN ALSTYNE
Music by PHOEBE P. KNAPP

CHURCH IN THE WILDWOOD

Words and Music by
WILLIAM S. PITTS

2. O come to the church in the wildwood,
To the trees where the wild flowers bloom;
Where the parting hymn will be changed,
We will weep by the side of the tomb.

3. From the church in the valley by the wildwood,
When day fades away into night,
I would fain from this spot of my childhood,
Wing my way to the mansions of light.

DO LORD

Traditional

Moderately fast

I've got a home in glory land that out-shines the sun.
I took Jesus as my Savior, you take Him too.

sun. I've got a home in glory land that
too. I took Jesus as my Savior,

out-shines the sun. I've got a home in glory land that
you take Him too. I took Jesus as my Savior,

GIVE ME THAT OLD TIME RELIGION

Traditional

Moderately bright

Chorus

Give Me That Old Time Re-li-gion; Give Me That Old Time Re-

li-gion. Give Me That Old Time Re-li-gion and it's good e-nough for

Verse

me. 1. It was good for the Proph-et Dan-iel; it was

2. It was good for Paul and Si-las, it was

3. It was good for old Abe Lincoln;
   It was good for old Abe Lincoln.
   It was good for old Abe Lincoln,
   And it's good enough for me.

GOD WILL TAKE CARE OF YOU

Words by CIVILLA D. MARTIN
Music by W. STILLMAN MARTIN

Be not dis - mayed ____ what - e'er be - tide;
Through days of toil ____ when heart doth fail;
All you may need ____ He will pro - vide;
No mat - ter what ____ may be the test,

God will take care of you. ____

Be - neath His wings ____ of
When dan - gers fierce ____ your
Noth - ing you ask ____ will
Lean, wea - ry one, ____ up -

HEAVENLY SUNLIGHT

Words by HENRY J. ZELLEY
Music by GEORGE HARRISON COOK

HIGHER GROUND

Words by JOHNSON OATMAN, JR.
Music by CHARLES H. GABRIEL

HIS EYE IS ON THE SPARROW

Text by CIVILLA D. MART
Music by CHARLES H. GABRI

JESUS, SAVIOR, PILOT ME

Words by EDWARD HOPPE
Music by JOHN E. GOUL

LEANING ON THE EVERLASTING ARMS

Words by ELISHA A. HOFFMAN
Music by ANTHONY J. SHOWALTER

I HAVE DECIDED TO FOLLOW JESUS

Words by an Indian Princ
Music by AUILA REA

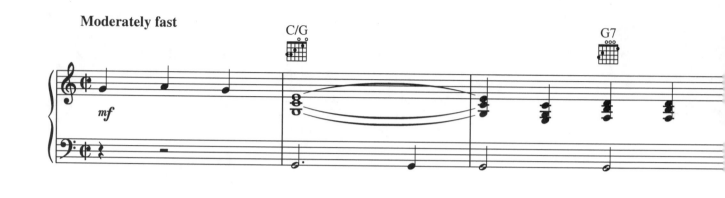

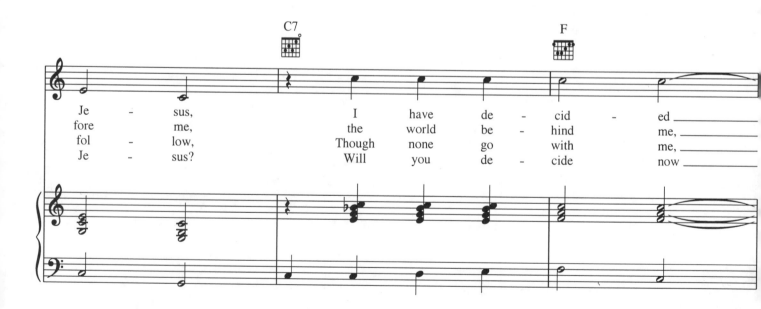

I'VE GOT PEACE LIKE A RIVER

Traditional

IN THE GARDEN

Words and Music
C. AUSTIN MIL...

SWEET BY AND BY

Words by SANFORD FILLMORE BENNE[T]
Music by JOSEPH P. WEBST[ER]

Cheerfully

There's a land that is fair - er than day,
and by
sing on that beau - ti - ful shore
the mel
boun - ti - ful Fa - ther a - bove
we will

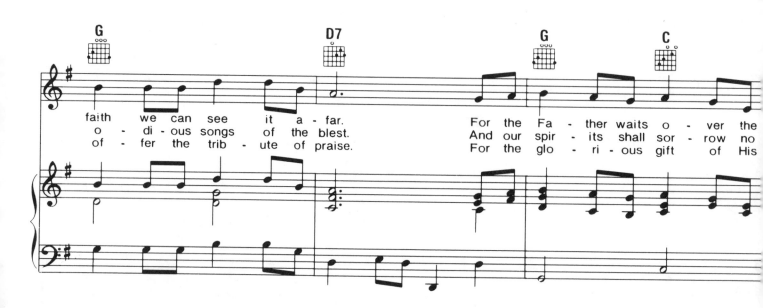

faith we can see it a - far.
For the Fa - ther waits o - ver the
o - di - ous songs of the blest.
And our spir - its shall sor - row no
of - fer the trib - ute of praise.
For the glo - ri - ous gift of His

JUST A CLOSER WALK WITH THEE

Traditional
Arranged by KENNETH MORRIS

JUST OVER IN THE GLORYLAND

Words and Music by J.W. ACUFF
and EMMETT DEAN

Additional Lyrics

2. I am on my way to those mansions fair,
   Just over in the gloryland;
   There to sing God's praise and His glory share,
   Just over in the gloryland.
   REFRAIN

3. What a joyful tho't that my Lord I'll see,
   Just over in the gloryland;
   And with kindred saved there forever be,
   Just over in the gloryland.
   REFRAIN

4. With the blood-washed throng I will shout and sing,
   Just over in the gloryland;
   Glad hosannas to Christ, the Lord and King,
   Just over in the gloryland.
   REFRAIN

LIFE'S RAILWAY TO HEAVEN

Words and Music by
M.E. ABBEY

43

THE LILY OF THE VALLEY

Words by CHARLES W. FRY
Music by WILLIAM S. HAYS

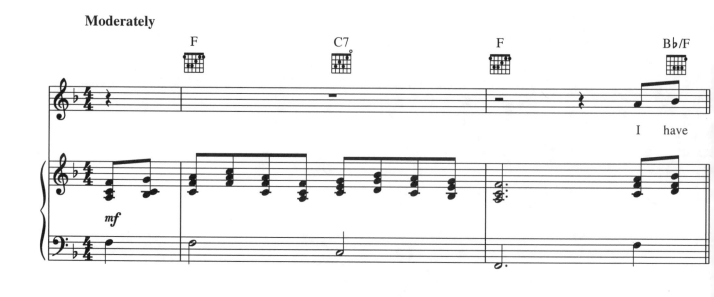

I have

found a friend in Je - sus, He's ev - 'ry - thing to me, He's the
all my grief has tak - en, and all my sor - rows borne; In temp -
nev - er, nev - er leave me, nor yet for - sake me here, While I

fair - est of ten - thou - sand to my soul; The ___ Lil - y of the Val - ley, in
ta - tion He's my strong and might - y tower; I have all for Him for - sak - en, and
live by faith and do His bless - ed will; A ___ wall of fire a - bout me, I've

MY SAVIOR FIRST OF ALL

Words by FANNY J. CROSBY
Music by JOHN R. SWENEY

NEARER MY GOD TO THEE

Text by SARAH F. ADAM
Music by LOWELL MASC

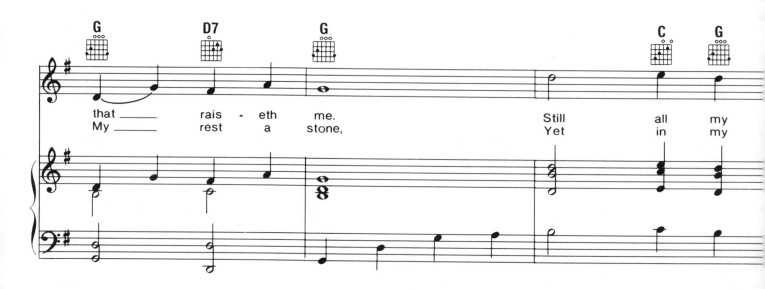

song   shall   be, Near - er my God, to Thee.
dreams   I'd   be,

Near - er, my God, to Thee, near - er to Thee!

3. Then with my waking tho'ts
   Bright with Thy praise,
   Out of my stony griefs
   Bethel I'll raise
   So by my woes to be,
   Nearer, my God, to Thee,
   Nearer, my God, to Thee,
   Nearer to Thee!

4. Or if on joyful wing,
   Cleaving the sky,
   Sun, moon, and stars forgot,
   Upwards I'll fly,
   Still all my song shall be,
   Nearer, my God, to Thee,
   Nearer, my God, to Thee,
   Nearer to Thee!

O, HOW I LOVE JESUS

Words by FREDERICK WHITFIELD
Traditional American Melody

PASS ME NOT, O GENTLE SAVIOR

Words by FANNY J. CROSBY
Music by WILLIAM H. DOANE

Additional Lyrics

2. Let me at the throne of mercy find a sweet relief;
   Kneeling there in deep contrition, help my unbelief.
   REFRAIN

3. Trusting only in Thy merit, would I seek Thy face;
   Heal my wounded, broken spirit, save me by Thy grace.
   REFRAIN

4. Thou, the Spring of all my comfort, more than life to me;
   Whom have I on earth beside Thee? Whom in heav'n but Thee?
   REFRAIN

WONDERFUL PEACE

Words by W.D. CORNELL
Music by W.G. COOPER

PRECIOUS MEMORIES

Words and Music by
J.B.F. WRIGHT

3. As I travel on life's pathway, I know not what life shall hold;
   As I wander hopes grow fonder, Precious mem'ries flood my soul.

REVIVE US AGAIN

Words and Music by WILLIAM MacKAY
and J.J. HUSBAND

ROCK OF AGES

Text by AUGUSTUS M. TOPLADY
Music by THOMAS HASTINGS

3. While I draw this fleeting breath
When my eyes shall close in death
When I rise to worlds unknown
And behold Thee on Thy throne
Rock of Ages cleft for me
Let me hide myself in Thee.

WHEN THE ROLL IS CALLED UP YONDER

Words and Music by
JAMES M. BLACK

When the trum-pet of the Lord shall sound and
bright and cloud-less morn-ing when the

time shall be no more, And the morn-ing breaks, e-ter-nal, bright and fair; When the
dead in Christ shall rise, And the glo-ry of His res-ur-rec-tion share; When His

saved of earth shall gath-er o-ver on the oth-er shore And the
cho-sen ones shall gath-er to their home be-yond the skies And the

SHALL WE GATHER AT THE RIVER?

Words and Music
ROBERT LOWRY

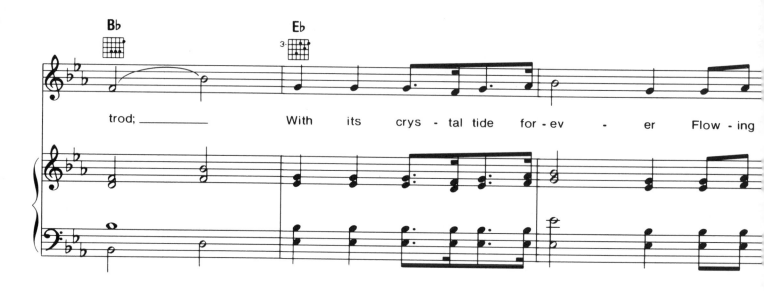

2. On the margin of the river,
   Washing up its silver spray,
   We shall walk and worship ever
   All the happy, golden day.

3. On the bosom of the river,
   Where the Saviour King we own,
   We shall meet and sorrow never
   'Neath the glory of the throne.

4. Ere we reach the shining river,
   Lay we ev'ry burden down:
   Grace our spirits will deliver,
   And provide a robe and crown.

5. Soon we'll reach the shining river,
   Soon our pilgrimage will cease;
   Soon our happy hearts will quiver
   With the melody of peace.

THERE IS A FOUNTAIN

Words by WILLIAM COWPER
Traditional American Melody
Arranged by LOWELL MASON

1. There _ is a foun-tain
2.-5. *(See additional lyrics)*

filled with blood Drawn _ from Im-man - uel's _ veins; And _

sin - ners, plunged be - neath that flood, Lose _ all their guilt - y stains: Lose _

69

Additional Lyrics

2. The dying thief rejoiced to see
   That fountain in his day;
   And there may I, though vile as he,
   Wash all my sins away:...

3. Dear dying Lamb, Thy precious blood
   Shall never lose its power,
   Till all the ransomed Church of God
   Be saved, to sin no more:...

4. E'er since by faith, I saw the stream
   Thy flowing wounds supply,
   Redeeming love has been my theme,
   And shall be till I die:...

5. Then in a nobler, sweeter song,
   I'll sing Thy power to save,
   When this poor lisping, stamm'ring tongue
   Lies silent in the grave:... Amen.

THERE IS POWER IN THE BLOOD

Words and Music by
LEWIS E. JONE

UNCLOUDED DAY

Words and Music by
J.K. ALWOOD

Moderately

O they

tell me of a home far be-yond the sky, O they tell me of a home far a-
tell me of a home where my friends have gone, O they tell me of a land far a-
tell me that He smiles on His chil-dren there, And His smile drives sor-rows all a-

way; Yes, they tell me of a home where no storm-clouds rise, O they
way; O they tell me of a tree in e-ter-nal bloom, O they
way; And they tell me that no heart-aches shall ev-er come, O that

WE'LL UNDERSTAND IT BETTER BY AND BY

Words and Music by
CHARLES A. TINDLEY

Additional Lyrics

2. We are often destitute of the things that life demands,
   Want of food and want of shelter, thirsty hills and barren lands,
   We are trusting in the Lord, and according to His word,
   We will understand it better by and by.
   REFRAIN

3. Trials dark on every hand, and we cannot understand,
   All the ways that God would lead us to that blessed Promised Land;
   But He guides us with His eye and we'll follow till we die,
   For we'll understand it better by and by.
   REFRAIN

4. Temptations, hidden snares often take us unawares,
   And our hearts are made to bleed for a thoughtless word or deed,
   And we wonder why the test when we try to do our best,
   But we'll understand it better by and by.
   REFRAIN

WHAT A FRIEND WE HAVE IN JESUS

Words by JOSEPH SCRIVE
Music by CHARLES C. CONVERS

Moderately

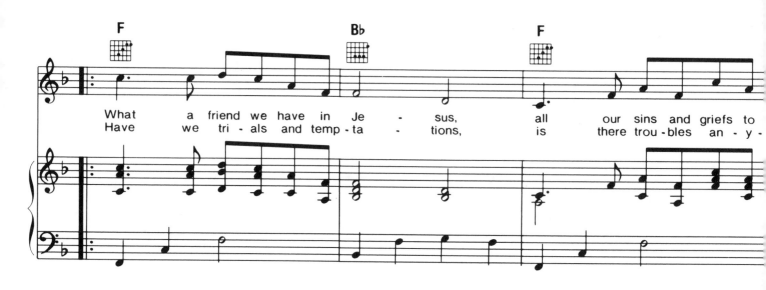

What a friend we have in Je - sus, all our sins and griefs to

Have we tri - als and temp - ta - tions, is there trou - bles an - y -

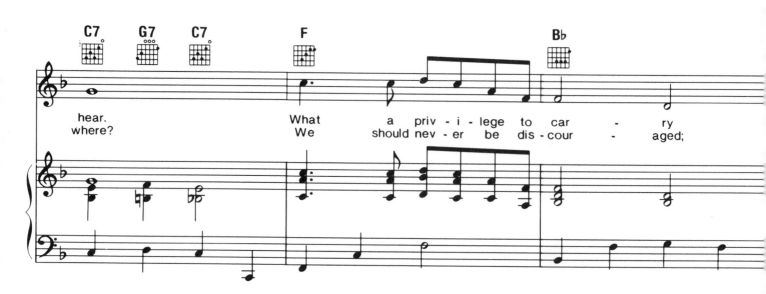

hear.
where?

What a priv - i - lege to car - ry

We should nev - er be dis - cour - aged;

3. Are we weak and heavy laden,
   cumbered with a load of care?
   Precious Savior still our refuge;
   take it to the Lord in prayer.
   Do thy friends despise, forsake thee?
   Take it to the Lord in prayer.
   In His arms He'll take and shield thee;
   thou will find a solace there.

WHEN WE ALL GET TO HEAVEN

Words and Music by E.E. HEWITT
and J.G. WILSON

1. Sing the won-drous
2.-4. *(See additional lyrics)*

love __ of __ Je - sus; Sing His mer - cy __ and His grace.

In the man - sions, bright and bless - ed, He'll pre - pare for us a

Additional Lyrics

2. While we walk the pilgrim pathway,
   Clouds will overspread the sky;
   But when trav'ling days are over,
   Not a shadow, not a sigh!
   REFRAIN

3. Let us then be true and faithful,
   Trusting, serving ev'ryday.
   Just one glimpse of Him in glory
   Will the toils of life repay.
   REFRAIN

4. Onward to the prize before us!
   Soon His beauty we'll behold.
   Soon the pearly gates will open;
   We shall tread the streets of gold.
   REFRAIN

WHISPERING HOPE

Words and Music b
ALICE HAWTHORN

WHITER THAN SNOW

Words by JAMES NICHOLSON
Music by WILLIAM G. FISCHER

1. Lord Je - sus, I long to be per - fect - ly whole; I
2.-4. *(See additional lyrics)*

want Thee for - ev - er to live in my soul, Break

down ev - ery i - dol, cast out ev - ery foe; Now

Additional Lyrics

2. Lord Jesus, look down from Thy throne in the skies,
    And help me to make a complete sacrifice;
    I give up myself, and whatever I know,
    Now wash me and I shall be whiter than snow.
    REFRAIN

3. Lord Jesus, for this I most humbly entreat,
    I wait, blessed Lord, at Thy crucified feet;
    By faith, for my cleansing I see Thy blood flow,
    Now wash me and I shall be whiter than snow.
    REFRAIN

4. Lord Jesus, Thou seeest I patiently wait,
    Come now, and within me a new heart create;
    To those who have sought Thee, Thou never saidst "No,"
    Now wash me and I shall be whiter than snow.
    REFRAIN

WONDERFUL GRACE OF JESUS

Tradition